What You Need to Know About

STOCKS

CORONA BREZINA AND BARBARA GOTTFRIED

Rosen
YA™
New York

Published in 2021 by The Rosen Publishing Group, Inc.
29 East 21st Street, New York, NY 10010

First Edition

Library of Congress Cataloging-in-Publication Data

Names: Brezina, Corona, author. | Gottfried, Barbara, author.
Title: What you need to know about stocks / Corona Brezina and Barbara Gottfried.
Description: First edition. | New York : Rosen Publishing, 2021. | Series:
The teen guide to adulting: gaining financial independence | Includes
bibliographical references and index. | Audience: Grades 7-12.
Identifiers: LCCN 2019022453 | ISBN 9781725340695 (library
binding) | ISBN 9781725340688 (paperback)
Subjects: LCSH: Stocks—Juvenile literature. | Investments—Juvenile literature.
Classification: LCC HG4661 .B74 2021 | DDC 332.63/22—dc23
LC record available at https://lccn.loc.gov/2019022453

Manufactured in China

CONTENTS

INTRODUCTION

Dan LaSalle, assistant principal at Olney Charter School in Philadelphia, Pennsylvania, has a modest goal for the students who participate in the school's personal finance program. According to MarketWatch.com, he wants every one of them to become millionaires later in their lives.

Students who participate in the program learn how to manage their money, from spending to saving to investing. They attend finance classes, but the real lessons come from hands-on experience. Students can earn real money working jobs within the school, such as tutoring or running clubs, and they deposit their money into checking or savings accounts opened through the program.

Some students also have investment accounts. LaSalle urges kids to invest in index funds, which contain stocks and other assets from a broad range of sectors. Students talk enthusiastically about their financial futures, including plans to invest in the stock market. Many joined the program for the opportunity to make money, but they ended up learning a lot more than they expected about financial responsibility, the path to wealth, and planning for their futures. Some students have already become entrepreneurs. The results are particularly impressive because Olney Charter School is a low-income school. Many parents lack a checking account themselves.

The students at Olney are lucky to have the opportunity to take a comprehensive personal finance course. Many

Students in Miami, Florida, participate in a personal finance class. Only seventeen states require that high school students take a course in personal finance.

young people report that high school didn't adequately prepare them to manage their personal finances. According to a 2019 survey, 68.5 percent of respondents wished that schools were required to teach stock market basics, as reported by the Motley Fool, a financial services company that provides advice to investors.

Financial literacy is essential to making the transition to adulthood, and understanding stocks and the stock market can be critical in planning your future financial security. Many people find the idea of investing in the stock market daunting—too risky for anyone other than wealthy, experienced investors. But as the Olney students demonstrate, charting your financial future can be empowering and even fun.

Stocks give investors the opportunity to buy ownership shares in companies. Companies benefit by obtaining capital, or money, to grow their businesses. Investors benefit by making a profit. Understanding how the stock market works can help you manage your own finances responsibly and recognize larger trends in the financial markets and world economy.

CHAPTER ONE

WHY OFFER STOCKS?

A corporation is a type of organization that can act as a legal entity separate from its owners. Like a person, a corporation has rights and responsibilities. Corporations can enter into contracts, borrow money, hire workers, pay taxes, and issue stocks. The corporation itself—not the shareholders—owns the company's assets, such as facilities and equipment, while management is separate from ownership. The shares owned by stockholders give them a stake in the company's profits. Corporations have limited liability, which means stockholders are not responsible for money owed by the company.

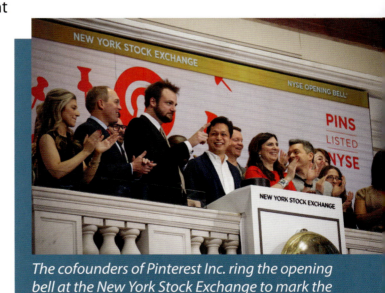

The cofounders of Pinterest Inc. ring the opening bell at the New York Stock Exchange to mark the tech company's initial public offering (IPO) on April 18, 2019.

Corporations begin when shareholders pursue a common goal, such as to earn profits or help a charitable cause. A board of directors for the corporation appoints and oversees people that deal with daily operations. Corporate laws create and regulate corporations.

WHO ISSUES STOCKS?

Corporations can be private or public. Private corporations have private ownership. They can issue stocks, but not through a public stock exchange. Public corporations issue stocks, or registered shares, through an exchange that allows stock buyers to trade with stock sellers.

A private company may choose to go public by putting stock shares up for sale on a public exchange. Offering shares through an exchange provides private corporations with opportunities to gain access to money from investors. Many private companies have a small number of shareholders, which may include the founders and employees as well as investors. When the corporation decides to go public, some portion of shares will be sold on public exchanges. Often, corporations that go from private to public are start-ups, which are relatively new businesses with the potential to grow quickly. In other cases, an established company may go public to seek funding to expand.

A primary offering happens when a private company goes public and registers with the Securities and Exchange Commission (SEC), the government agency that oversees markets and protects investors' interests. This stock offering—

the first time the corporation issues stock—is also known as initial public offering (IPO). After issuing a primary offering, the newly public companies can also make secondary offerings, which allow for even more outstanding shares in the market. ("Outstanding" means owned by shareholders.)

Since the early 1990s, many of the most hyped IPOs have been tech companies going from private to public. In 2012, for example, Facebook raised $16 billion through its IPO, one of the largest in history, according to CNN. The funds allowed

Companies preparing for an IPO are required to file disclosure documents about their financial condition and business practices with the Securities and Exchange Commission (SEC), headquartered in Washington, DC.

the company to acquire other tech services and recruit top computer engineers and directors. Two of the most highly anticipated IPOs of 2019 were car service companies Lyft and Uber. Lyft was valued at $24.3 billion ahead of its April IPO, in which it raised $2.34 billion, according to VentureBeat. Uber was expected to debut with a much larger IPO.

The names of many of the biggest public corporations are instantly recognizable. They include major companies such as Apple, Alphabet (the parent company of Google), Microsoft, Johnson & Johnson, Wal-Mart Stores, AT&T, and Amazon. The list of the most profitable public companies often includes energy companies, such as ExxonMobil and Royal Dutch Shell, and financial service companies, such as JPMorgan Chase, Bank of America, and Visa.

News about Facebook's IPO is displayed on the NASDAQ stock exchange in New York on May 18, 2012, the date that the tech giant began trading publicly.

WHAT YOU NEED TO KNOW ABOUT STOCKS

WHY DO COMPANIES ISSUE STOCKS?

Equity financing refers to investors gaining part ownership of a company in exchange for payment to the company. The ownership is represented by the stock. Companies use the stock payment to help their businesses grow. Consider a company that sells T-shirts. The demand for the shirts is growing. This company can earn more profits by increasing its shirt production. Profits are the money left over after costs are subtracted from revenue (money earned). To increase production, the T-shirt company needs to purchase more

PREFERRED OR COMMON STOCK

Most stocks issued by corporations are classified as either common stock or preferred stock. Both types represent ownership shares of a corporation. The main differences between these two stocks consist of voting rights and dividends. Voting rights gives shareholders a voice in company decisions. Dividends are money paid to shareholders out of the company profits.

Investors usually own common stocks, which give shareowners the right to vote. Common stocks are dependent on the company's performance and may or may not pay dividends. Preferred stocks generally do not allow voting rights, but they provide regularly paid dividends that are not tied to a company's earnings. Preferred stock is often described as a combination between common stock and a bond (a type of investment that provides a fixed income).

equipment and inputs (like cotton) and to pay additional workers. Issuing stocks provides the money to buy these things.

Corporations use money from stocks to acquire factors of production, which include capital, land, labor, and entrepreneurship. These factors are used to make goods and services whose sales earn profits. Capital refers to buying goods used to increase production, such as equipment. Land includes actual land, office buildings, factories, and natural resources (such as oil). Another factor, labor, consists of the people who produce goods and services for sale. Corporations pay workers

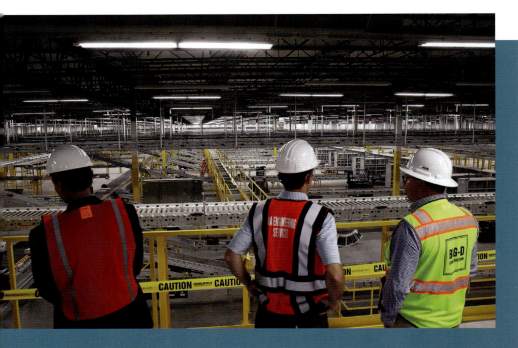

Workers view a conveyor belt system on the floor of a 855,000-square-foot Amazon fulfillment center under construction in Sacramento, California. The company expected to hire 1,500 workers at the facility.

in wages, such as $15 per hour, or salaries, like $50,000 each year. Human capital includes skilled workers who receive higher pay. Entrepreneurship refers to the way all the other factors are brought together for production.

A corporation may issue stocks to pay for factors of production that allow for the business to grow. If expanding, corporations may launch further into domestic markets or expand into foreign ones. A corporation may also choose to use money raised by issuing stocks to offer new products or build new facilities. Another way that corporations gather money for their costs is called debt-financing. This method involves borrowing money from institutions like banks by offering bonds. Businesses can also issue stocks to pay off debts, or money owed.

Corporations can also issue stocks to obtain money for mergers or acquisitions. A merger joins two existing companies into a single new company. Mergers occur to gain market share (or a bigger part of the marketplace for a certain good or service), lower business costs, increase profits, and expand into new markets. Shareholders of both companies get stocks in the new corporation.

An acquisition takes place when a corporation buys most or all of another company's shares. Corporations can acquire another company with cash, stock, or a combination of both. The buying company purchases at least 50 percent of the other company. A corporation may make an acquisition to lower the costs of a company or to gain more market share. Acquisitions can also improve a company's performance through economies of scale. Using the advantages of

OPTIONS FOR GOING PUBLIC

Most private corporations go public by offering an IPO. A less commonly used process is called a Direct Public Offering (DPO). An IPO is managed by an investment bank, which charges millions of dollars for the service. New stock shares are issued and sold to the public. A certain amount of revenue is guaranteed through the process. During a DPO, the company sells stock directly to buyers rather than working with an investment bank. Only existing shares owned by founders, employees, and early investors are sold to the public. The process is less expensive and faster than an IPO, but it can also be riskier. The stock price is influenced by market demand, or the factors that affect the willingness and ability to buy the stock.

In April 2018, the tech music company Spotify became the biggest company to go public using a DPO, achieving a $26.5 billion valuation, according to *Fortune*. Unlike many companies that opt to go public, Spotify did not aim to raise capital through the process. Spotify's going public did provide other advantages, such as allowing its existing investors and employees to trade their shares on the market. As a successful, high-profile company, Spotify was in a stronger position than many other start-ups to pursue a successful DPO without relying on an investment bank to provide support and generate publicity through an IPO.

economies of scale means that companies save on costs by making more of their products, comparable to buying in bulk. Buyers buy more of an item to get a lower cost per item.

DECISIONS, DECISIONS

Consider a new company that needs to raise capital for its operations. It has two options: to borrow money, such as a loan through the bank, or to issue stocks. For the first option, a bank, or another lending institution, uses credit ratings to determine whether to provide a loan. A credit rating allows lenders to assess the probability that a borrower will repay the loan. The higher the credit rating, the greater the chance that the borrower will repay money that is borrowed. If a company does not have a strong credit rating, then it is harder for a company to obtain the money it needs. But, this same corporation can instead issue stocks to try to obtain needed capital.

Executives at Match Group Inc., owner of online-dating services, open the trading day at the NASDAQ on November 20, 2015, the day after its IPO.

Corporations' main goals are to maximize their profits, or money earned after paying costs. Investors want to put their money into companies that they predict will earn them more money. When assessing companies, investors look at the amount of debt a company owes. Greater debt can mean that a company is a riskier investment, and discourage investors from putting their money into the company. Borrowing money creates more debt. But issuing stocks does not.

When a corporation is established, it has articles of incorporation, a document that specifies the maximum amount of shares that the business can offer. A corporation may choose not to issue this full amount all at once. This decision gives it the option of issuing more stocks, or raising more capital, at a future date. When a corporation issues stocks, or shares in the company, it decides how much capital it needs. Then it can figure out how many stocks to offer. A company can determine a target share price based on an estimate of the fair value of the company. The fair value is the sale price of the company that both a buyer and seller would agree upon in the marketplace.

When determining a price for each share, a corporation takes into account that each stock represents an ownership part. Consider a new company that aims to raise $500,000. It issues 5,000 stocks for $100 per each share. An investor who has 2,500 shares worth $100 apiece owns 50 percent of the stock offered to the public. The lower the share price, the less each share represents in the corporation. If each share were instead worth $50, the company would have to issue more shares to raise the target sum of $500,000, and an investor with 2,500 shares only owns 25 percent of the total.

LET'S DO IT

There are advantages and disadvantages to going public. A company incurs costs during the process, such as fees charged by investment banks. An IPO is a long process that can distract management from the business of running the company. The company may also not grow as quickly in the months after the IPO. And by offering stock to more people, owners relinquish some control of the company. The new shareholders may put pressure on the company to maximize short-term profits rather than long-term performance.

But offering stocks to the public also helps a company gain more access to money for future expansion. This growth can include investing in more equipment, hiring more workers, and even acquiring other companies. Going public also creates publicity and can open up new opportunities.

After a company decides to offer stock to the public, it can begin preparing for an IPO. About six months in advance, the company selects an investment bank and begins filing financial information with the SEC. The bank and company leaders then seek out the interest of major prospective investors during a "road show"—they aim to attract more demand for the stock than they will be able to fill. They then decide how many shares to issue and an offering price for the shares, which depends on the success of the road show and general economic conditions.

Following the IPO, the company will appear on the stock exchange listing. It will be expected to follow new rules about the reporting and disclosure of financial information that are required of publicly traded companies.

2 LET'S INVEST

A market is made up of consumers and businesses that exchange goods and services based on supply and demand. Stocks are bought and sold during transactions on the stock market. Corporations supply stock for various reasons, such as raising money to expand operations or open new facilities. Investors provide the demand for these stocks, buying stocks that they believe will yield a return, or make money for them. But there is no guarantee that a stock will meet expectations. Investors can lose money if the stock price falls. Anyone considering investing in stocks must acknowledge that there is an element of risk. It's important to learn

Stockbrokers and traders buy and sell stocks on the floor of the New York Stock Exchange. Founded in 1792, it is the world's largest stock exchange.

about the factors that indicate whether or not a stock is a potentially good investment when making the decision to buy.

There are two primary ways that investors make money through stocks. These include dividends and capital appreciation.

REAPING THE DIVIDENDS

Companies that make solid earnings may distribute some of the profits in the form of dividends. A company's revenue is money earned from sales of its goods and services. Companies also pay costs associated with making their products. When costs are subtracted from revenue, the result is profit. Most of the profits are used to help the company continue to grow. But part of a company's profits can be paid out to shareholders in the form of dividends. A dividend yield is a dividend as percentage of current stock price. These dividends can be given to shareholders

Shareholders own stock in a company and have voting rights regarding certain corporate issues, but they are not involved in day-to-day management.

in different ways: cash, stocks, or other forms such as property. Cash is the most popular!

Companies that pay regular dividends are sometimes known as income stocks, because they generate a consistent yield for investors. Not all stock investments pay out dividends. Larger, older companies are more likely to offer dividends at regular times. Start-up companies may have a greater need to put all their profits into growth so they may not pay out regular dividends to their shareholders. High-growth companies (those that increase in size quickly and are expected to perform better than other companies in their industry) may also not offer regular dividends because they have significant costs related to expansion that require all of their profits.

Investors who expect to receive dividends should be aware of the calendar for key dates. Companies report quarterly earnings, meaning four times a year, and decide at this point whether or not to pay dividends to shareholders. The announcement date (also called a declaration date) is when the company announces the dividend payments. The payment date is when the company pays out dividends to stockholders. An investor must own the stock for a certain number of days before being eligible to receive dividends.

When investors receive dividends, it can instill confidence in the company. On the flip side, if a company decides to reduce their dividends, then investors may view their investment negatively. In 2017, for example, General Electric company (GE) decided to cut its dividends by 50 percent and its stock prices fell by more than 7 percent, according to CNBC.

BUY LOW, SELL HIGH

A stock is an investment. People put their money into stocks because they want to earn money. Stock prices tend to vary rather than rise or fall continuously. These changes affect when an investor decides to buy or sell stocks.

Consider an investor who has an opportunity to buy a stock that costs $10 per share. She believes that the price of the stock will increase to $50 per share. She buys 100 shares and holds onto this stock for a certain amount of time. During that time, the stock price fluctuates—moves up and down. It changes from the $10 value.

The value of this investor's stock changes over time. When the investor bought the stock, she bought $1,000 worth of shares. If the stock price rises to $12 per share, this investor's stocks increase to $1,200. If the stock price falls to $7 per share, they drop to $700. This does not mean that the change in stock price automatically earned the investor $200 when it rose or lost the investor $300 when it fell.

An investor only gains or loses money on a stock investment when the stock is sold. Suppose the investor's hopes are realized and the stock price increases to $50 per share. If the investor sold the stock then, she earned $4,000 on her investment ($5,000 value when sold minus $1,000 value when bought).

The general rule for stock investments is "buy low, sell high." Investors look to buy stocks with low prices and then sell them when the price is higher. "Buy low" is like buying a good or service on sale. It's a deal! Selling the stock when its price increases means that the investor earns money on the sale.

APPLE (AAPL)
171.22 -1.58 [-0.91%] • EXT HOURS

1-YR [20.20%]

195
180
165
150
135

M J J A S O N D J F M A

171.22

A chart shown in April of 2018 shows Apple's stock price over the period of a year, the recent decline reflecting a possible drop in smartphone demand.

With some stocks, investors can earn money quickly. With other stocks, investors may hold the stock for a while before earning money from a sale. Other times, investors may lose money on their stock investments, because they may choose to sell their stock when the price is lower than what they paid for it.

Stocks chosen for their potential to increase in value are known as growth stocks. Making money by buying stocks and selling them for a higher price is known as capital appreciation, or capital gains. The increase in price is called a return. The return is expressed as a percentage—the investor discussed previously who earned $4,000 on a $1,000 investment had a 400 percent return. If an investor receives dividends from a stock as well as capital gains upon its sale, the combination is called total return.

WHAT SHOULD I CHOOSE?

Investors want to earn money on stocks. The challenge is in identifying stocks that are likely to increase in value over time. There is no guarantee that the stock prices will rise. But there are factors that might help an investor to feel more confident about potential returns.

There are some basic strategies for choosing stocks. First, look for stocks with low prices. Depending on the company, these stocks may be more likely to increase over time. Second, an investor may consider buying shares in a certain company when a stock price hits a certain value or range of values. For example, an investor may be interested in a company and want to buy its shares when the stock price is between $10 and $12.

Third, stock investors look for companies with solid expected growth. These companies are more likely to earn money for the investors, like dividends, stock gains, or both. Fourth, some companies are undervalued. Investors look at factors such as the stock's price and dividend yield as well as the company's assets, debts, and earnings. This type of data is often expressed in measurements, such as ratios and statistics, which experienced investors can assess to forecast future performance.

Companies that investors regularly shop may also be considered as good stock investments for ordinary individuals looking for stocks. Investors check out the company's position, like profit margin and the breakdown of revenues and expenses. How much money does a company owe? More debt

STOCKS AND TEEN TRENDSETTERS

Teens are known as savvy trendsetters who are the first to spot the newest exciting fashions, social media services, and activities. Believe it or not, teen trends can even have implications for the stock market. Companies make money when consumers buy their products and services. This increase in revenue can be reflected in stock prices. Often, trends that begin with teens can grow into widespread popularity. When consumers are expected to buy more of a product or service, investors may look at the parent company as a good potential investment.

Some investors look to teens and their trends for buying power. So, what do teens buy? A 2018 *U.S. News and World Report* survey of more than 8,000 American teens found that places like Chipotle Mexican Grill, Starbucks, Nike, VF Corporation (parent company of the Vans brand), Amazon.com, Facebook, Apple, and Netflix topped the list.

can make share prices more volatile—frequently changing by significant amounts—as companies use earnings to pay off debt and interest, which is the cost of borrowing money.

Investors should be warned, however, that there may be a reason that a certain stock price is very low. Before putting money into shares, conscientious investors investigate a company with a low stock price to find out whether they believe that the price is likely to rise. Penny stocks, for example, are stocks issued by small companies that trade for less than $5 per share. Some investors are attracted to these stocks because of high potential for growth, but penny stocks are very risky investments. Many companies that issue penny stocks fail to grow or go out of business.

BULL OR BEAR MARKET

Markets can be called "bull" or "bear" depending on performance. Bull markets occur when prices, usually in the stock market, are expected to rise or are already rising over a certain amount of time. These market trends can last for months or years. During a bull market, investors are confident in the market, and they are eager to jump in and invest. Investors try to figure out the peak for a stock—the stock's high price before it begins to fall.

A bull market generally occurs during periods marked by overall economic growth, low unemployment, rising corporate earnings, and strong investor confidence.

Suppose an investor buys a stock at $10 per share. The investor wants to earn the most money she can. It's a bull market and prices are rising. Her stock is now worth $12 per share and soon $20 per share. Should she sell? She can double her money at $20 per share. But if her stock increases to $40 per share, she could make even more money! Will the stock increase that much? It can be challenging for investors to tell where a stock will peak.

But during a bear market, the opposite trends occur. In general, a bear market is characterized by at least a 20 percent overall drop in stock prices for two months or more, according to Motley Fool. When prices fall, investors are nervous about putting their money into assets, like stocks, that may lose value. Some investors may get good deals as stock prices can be on their way down. Overall, however, making investments is risky during a bear market. Investors tend to sell to avoid losing more money, which contributes to a cycle of falling prices. Trading activity slows and dividends tend to drop. Eventually, investors begin to take advantage of the low stock prices, investor confidence begins to increase, and conditions move back to a bull market.

MYTHS & FACTS

MYTH   **Investing in stocks is too risky unless you're a financial expert.**

Fact   *Although buying stocks does carry risk, ordinary individuals can receive sound advice on investing in stocks from investment advisors, brokerages, and online investing services. The stock market does fluctuate over the short term, but it has been proven to yield solid returns over the long-term.*

MYTH   **The best way to make money on the stock market is to put your money in stocks issued by a company that looks like a sure bet for growth.**

Fact   *No single stock can be guaranteed to succeed, and it's very risky to invest all of your money in the same place. Experts recommend that investors diversify by putting their money into various types of assets, which can include a mixture of different stocks.*

MYTH   **Volatility in the price of one of my stocks is a troublesome sign, and it might be a good decision to sell.**

Fact   *Short-term volatility doesn't reflect long-term market performance. Investors shouldn't make decisions based solely on day-to-day price fluctuations.*

CHAPTER THREE

TO BUY OR NOT TO BUY

O nce you've decided to invest in stocks, the next step is to assess your own goals and financial situation. Do you want to buy stocks that will yield dividends or appreciate in value? Is the timing right to buy the stocks that interest you—is the price likely to continue rising? How long do you want to hold onto your stocks? Have you determined a price range in which you'll sell your stocks?

Your financial and personal situation is also relevant to your investment choices. Young people are often more likely to make risky investments, for example. An older investor may be unwilling to risk

An inexperienced investor may encounter a wide variety of stock market investment choices. Expert advice and background research can help craft a winning investment strategy.

losing money on the stock market if it could affect his or her retirement savings. Younger investors may be more confident that long-term gains will make up for short-term losses. Make sure that your personal finances are in order before you invest. If you owe any high-interest debt, you should pay that off before putting money in stocks. It's also responsible to have some money put aside in savings.

Teens who are interested in investing may choose stocks using the same means as other investors, but they can consider drawing on resources closer to home as well. If relatives work for corporations, for example, maybe they can share their opinions on trends in those industries. Teens can also investigate stocks related to their hobbies and interests. A sports fanatic may start out by researching sports-related companies. Young investors may also join school or community investment clubs where they can discuss investment tips and techniques with peers.

When you're ready to buy, you must make practical decisions on making transactions. Buying and selling stocks can involve third parties and opening an account to keep cash or stocks. Investors often buy stocks through brokerages or online sites.

STOCK BASICS

When investing, it helps to be familiar with certain terms and measurements that investors use in discussing stocks. If you're looking at a specific company, you can learn about its financial condition by reviewing its statements, including its balance sheet, cash flow statement, and income statement.

One important measurement in evaluating a stock's value is the price-to-earnings (P/E) ratio, which looks at the price paid for each dollar a company earns. The P/E ratio indicates how expensive a stock is. It is calculated as the price per share divided by the earnings per share. This measure is directly related to profits. A company with zero profits has a zero P/E ratio, while a high P/E ratio indicates high value.

The P/E ratio can be figured out for each stock. For example, on a specific day a company reports earnings per share of $3 and its stock sells for $30 per share, so the P/E ratio is 10 ($30 price per share divided by $3 earnings per share = 10 P/E). A savvy investor should compare that figure to the P/E ratios of similar companies in the industry. A lower P/E ratio in the range indicates greater earning power and a better potential investment.

According to Adam Hayes on Investopedia, the P/E ratio indicates what the market is prepared to pay for a stock based on that stock's past or future earnings. If the P/E ratio of the stock is high, that could show that the stock's price is possibly overvalued because it is high relative to earnings. A low P/E ratio could show that the stock price is low relative to earnings. Some stocks with a low P/E ratio are known as value stocks, and investors buy them in the hope that they are undervalued and their price will rise.

Earnings per share (EPS) is a measurement that can indicate a company's growth. It is calculated as the earnings divided by the average number of stock shares outstanding. Higher EPS values may indicate to investors that the company has been making a profit and has money to expand its business operations or distribute as dividends.

Return on equity (ROE) is another measurement of a stock's performance that reflects its profits. It indicates how much money a stock has made off of shareholders' investments in the company. The figure is a percentage—any amount above 20 percent represents a good return. If the figure is negative, the shareholders are losing value.

These metrics—P/E ratio, EPS, and ROE—are only a few of the many measurements that can be used to evaluate stocks. Each has its limitations, and it's best to consider several different metrics for a particular stock and also compare the measurements to those of other companies within an industry.

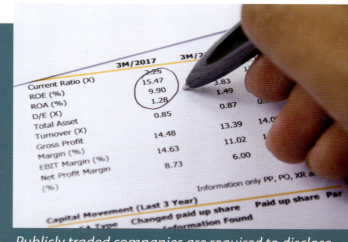

Publicly traded companies are required to disclose certain financial reports and information about operations so that potential investors can make informed investment decisions.

Stock market capitalization—or market cap—is another important factor in choosing stocks. Market cap is the total value of all of the company's stock shares. It is calculated by multiplying the number of shares by the market price of a share. A stock can be small, mid, or large cap, and each carries a different amount of risk and potential returns. According to The Balance, large-cap stocks are $10 billion or more; mid cap are between $2 billion and $10 billion; and small cap are between $250 million and $2 billion. Market cap figures provide an easy means of comparing the sizes of different companies.

Many small-cap companies are start-ups that have good potential for growth but are also high risk. Large-cap

Stocks in large cap companies such as Apple Inc. (headquartered in Cupertino, California) offer investors stable, safe investments that are likely to pay out dividends.

companies, by contrast, are solidly established and carry less risk but may expect a slower growth rate.

Blue chip stocks are those issued by huge companies that are reliable and well-established. They generally experience steady growth and pay dividends for investors. Many are companies with instantly recognizable names, such as Disney, IBM, and Goldman Sachs.

A company can decide to split its stock by increasing the number of shares and reducing the value of each share. If you own 100 shares of stock worth $160 apiece and the stock splits 2-for-1, you will subsequently own 200 shares worth $80 apiece. The total value of your shares does not change. A company

INVESTMENT PHILOSOPHY

An investment philosophy is a set of principles and practices that guide an investor's decisions. Having a coherent investment philosophy can help an investor focus on long-term goals and avoid falling for market fads or panicking over short-term losses. An investment philosophy can include how long you want to hold onto stocks or how much risk you can handle. It may involve avoiding certain strategies or periodically rebalancing your portfolio—buying and selling stocks or other assets to maintain a certain combination of different types. Some investors choose to invest in socially responsible companies, even if it means passing up on promising opportunities that don't meet their criteria.

There's no single perfect investment philosophy. Investors should develop an investment philosophy that suits their own financial circumstances, goals, and temperament.

may split its stock in the belief that investors will be more likely to buy shares at the lower price. The move can be viewed as a positive sign, because it indicates that the company anticipates high demand from investors.

STOCKBROKERS 911

Most investors do not buy stocks directly from companies. Stockbrokers (also called share brokers) are experts who help potential investors to navigate the stock market. Some

Stockbrokers carry out an investor's trades on the stock market. Many brokerages offer broker services as well as investing tools and research on individual stocks available online.

brokerage firms provide stockbroker services for investors to manage their stocks. If using a broker, investors specify quantity and kind of stock. A stockbroker performs the stock transaction and then takes a payment, called a trade commission, in return. This commission is often a percentage of the share.

Today, investors have a variety of options regarding how they buy and sell stocks. Full-service brokers take time to know their investors so they can help them make financial plans for the future. Clients are also paying for the firm's expertise in recommending stocks—many firms have a research branch that evaluates which stocks are likely to perform well. Online or discount brokers simply execute the client's trades, so their fees are less than full-service ones. Cost is based on transaction. Investors who trade through discount brokers are responsible for their own investment strategies and must conduct more research when choosing stocks. Individuals can also invest directly into companies through a Direct Stock Purchase Plan (DSPP), where transactions are conducted through transfer agents rather than brokers.

There are many fees, commissions, and charges associated with stock market transactions, and they vary from one brokerage to another. If you are trading stocks, find a broker with a low trade commission.

BROKERAGE ACCOUNTS

A brokerage account is set up to conduct investments. The application takes about twenty minutes to complete, and most states have an age limit of eighteen. Parents can open an account for children less than this age under the Uniform Gift to Minors Act or Uniform Transfer to Minors Act. At the age of eighteen or twenty-one (depending on the state), children can then take full control of their accounts.

Different companies may offer the same account with different fees and required minimum amounts. One investment firm may have a $100 minimum for a custodial account (which a parent opens for his or her child) while another firm may set a $2,500 minimum.

Investors use funds in a brokerage account to buy and sell stocks as well as other investments, such as bonds. Online brokerage accounts allow investors to handle transactions via online trading platforms. Other brokerage accounts come with human managers to help with investments or robo-advisers, which are online automated versions at a lower cost. A robo-adviser can also build your portfolio, which is a combination of investment tools.

WHAT'S THE ORDER?

An investor has various options when placing orders to buy or sell stock. A stock has bid and ask prices. The sell price for a stock is the bid price. The buy price for the stock is the ask price. The spread is the difference between the highest bid price and the lowest ask price. A market order is when an investor buys a stock at the current market price. Bid and ask prices change throughout the day. A market order can take place immediately, but there still might be a difference in the ask price that was quoted minutes before! A limit order can be made to buy a stock at a specific price. If an investor requests a bid price of $50 and the stock price is $55, the broker will wait until the price hits $50 before buying.

Which order is right for an investor? If the priority for the investor is to carry out the stock transaction, then the market order is appropriate because it happens immediately.

Investment clubs can provide great opportunities for teens to learn from each other as they explore ways to manage money, research stocks, and follow economic trends.

If getting the right ask price is most important, the limit order is the better option. Market orders are performed first and then limit orders take place if the ask price still matches the current market price.

When making stock transactions, be mindful of the fees. Investment and brokerage fees take away from the returns earned by stock orders.

STAY CURRENT

Savvy investors stay informed on the latest business and finance trends. There are many news sources that provide information on the market and specific companies and stocks. What mergers are happening? What acquisitions occurred recently? What are the latest consumer fads? How are current events affecting company costs? Corporate press releases also give information on the health and future prospects of companies.

The price of oil offers an example of how staying current helps investing. Most companies are reliant on oil. For example, oil heats offices, fuels trucks that deliver products to stores, and provides energy to run machines. When oil prices increase, then a major cost for many companies also increases. This increase can be reflected in higher prices paid by consumers.

If a product's price increases, then the demand for the product most likely will decrease. This consequence means higher costs with fewer sales, which can decrease company profits and make its stock less attractive as an investment. Investors who anticipate the effects of rising input prices can also make more informed decisions about their investments.

10 GREAT QUESTIONS

TO ASK A FINANCIAL SPECIALIST

1 How do I choose the right stock?

2 If I want to earn money, how long should I hold my stocks before selling them?

3 Are there certain kinds of stocks that earn more money?

4 What criteria do I use to choose a stock?

5 How do I open a brokerage account?

6 What kind of brokerage accounts are available to me?

7 How much do you charge for stock transactions?

8 How risky are stock investments?

9 How can I figure out my personal investment philosophy?

10 Do I pay taxes on my stock investments?

4 ENTER AT YOUR OWN RISK

I nvestors are attracted to the stock market by the potential for higher returns than the interest from savings accounts or the fixed return from bonds. But when an investor chooses to buy stocks to achieve greater rewards, he or she must also accept that there's a greater risk of losing money. An individual's investment style can be categorized as conservative (or risk averse), moderate, or aggressive (willing to take risks). No investor can completely insulate himself or herself from risk, even the experts. The financial markets can be affected by outside events and pressures that are impossible to predict.

RISKY INVESTMENTS

Each type of investment carries different risks and returns. Consider a bond that pays a fixed amount each month. Bonds carry low risk, because investors can feel secure that they will receive this fixed amount. Many individual stocks, or tools that include stocks, earn more money than bonds but they also carry more risk. This risk comes from the idea that the investor can lose more money than she originally invested. Generally, the higher the risk, the higher the potential return.

Risk from stock investments can come from many sources, such as economic or political events. Consider an economic or political event that raises oil prices. When the price of oil increases, costs for companies become more expensive. They have to pay more to transport their goods across the country to stores, for example. This increase in costs is then passed along to the consumer, who may cut back on buying the company's products. When people buy

In March of 2019, Brazil's stock market reacted negatively to the news that the nation's former president Michel Temer had been arrested during a wide-ranging corruption probe.

fewer of a company's products over time, the company's stock prices may fall.

Volatility, or market risk, refers to changes in a stock's price over time. Stock prices continually fluctuate, but the price movement of highly volatile stocks is more frequent and extreme. Volatility tends to make investors nervous. Selling a volatile stock at a low point can result in a loss. On the other hand, some investors buy when the price is low in the hope of making a higher return. Many investors, however, disregard

HOW RISKY ARE YOU?

An individual's investment strategy depends largely on his or her attitude toward risk. The most obvious risk to an investor is losing money when an asset fails to deliver returns. But there are specific types of risk associated with investing in stocks. Investor.gov lists a few different areas of risks that investors should take into consideration. There's a business risk, for example—the company you own stock in could go bankrupt, potentially leaving investors with nothing. Volatility risk involves stock prices fluctuating significantly. Changes in interest rates and inflation levels in the economy can also affect prices and returns of some types of assets.

Investment risk is usually related to returns—the higher the risk, the greater the potential return. Experts often advise on minimizing risk, but some investors have a higher tolerance for risk than others. Risk averse investors may choose stocks that are considered safer. Investors who are more willing to opt for high-risk stocks should research individual companies thoroughly and gain experience on the stock market before making risky buys.

a stock's short-term volatility in the expectation that it will average out to a solid long-term performance.

DIVERSIFY

Have you heard the expression, "Don't put all of your eggs in one basket?" It refers to storing all of one's resources in the same place. Suppose an investor has $1,000 to invest. He puts

Asset allocation is a strategy that allows an investor to control risk by dividing investments among different types of assets, resulting in a diversified portfolio.

puts all his money in one stock. The investor buys 20 shares of the ABC Company at $50 per share. The ABC Company does poorly and the stock is now only worth $10 per share. Now, the investor's $1,000 investment is worth only $200.

Another investor, with $1,000 to invest, decides to put half of her money into the ABC Company. She buys 10 shares at $50 per share. She then invests the other half of her money into the XYZ Corporation. With that company, she buys 25 shares at $20 per share. In time, the ABC Company's stock is worth only $100 from the original $500 investment. But the XYZ Corporation does financially well and her original investment of $500 is now worth $750. The first investor had $1,000 and now only has $200. The second investor had $1,000 and now has $850. In this case, the second investor's stocks fared better, because she invested in two different companies that had very different returns.

By investing in different companies, the second investor increased the potential of gaining a positive return. If one company did not do well, she could still potentially earn money from her investment in another company. Many investors choose to differentiate, or diversify, their investments in hopes of earning greater returns by spreading them out among different types of assets. Asset allocation is a mix of stocks, bonds, and other assets within an investment portfolio. It may include stocks carrying varying levels of risk drawn from a variety of different industries. This strategy allows an investor to recoup potential losses, or at least offset some of them, if some investments do not earn as

BEST STOCKS FROM 2007–2017

Some investors made fantastic returns over a period of ten years by choosing stocks that increased very rapidly in value. Consider the movie rental company Netflix. In ten years, the stock rose in value by almost 5,000 percent! A person investing $400 in 2007 could have bought 100 shares of Netflix stock for $4 each. By 2017, this person could have sold the stock for $500,000! Other companies with stocks that rose over 4,000 percent included commercial laundry and dry cleaning equipment corporation EnviroStar, Inc. and Gtt Communications, a telecommunications and internet service provider company.

much as expected. Generally, different types of assets do not rise and fall in value in sync with each other. If stock values fall sharply, bond returns may compensate for some of the loss.

POOLING IT

To diversify, investors may choose to buy mutual funds. A mutual fund is a portfolio that can include a combination of stocks, bonds, and other types of investments. This tool allows investors to put their money into several places that carry different potential returns and risk. With a mutual fund, an investor may lose money on some of the stocks making up the fund, but then gain money on the part of the fund that includes bonds. The average mutual fund has hundreds of different securities.

Mutual funds are compiled by professional fund managers. Individual investors buy shares of mutual funds, and the pool of money is used to invest in a large group of assets. Profits are shared among the investors. There are many advantages to mutual funds. They are an easy investment and are affordable for small investors. Mutual funds are a diversified investment. As with any investment, the risk level, performance, and goals vary from one mutual fund to another. They may pay dividends, yield capital gains, or increase in value.

Investors can buy mutual funds through a brokerage or, in some cases, directly from the fund. Check the fees involved with the fund—there will be initial fees as well as ongoing fees and expenses that vary from one mutual fund to another. Generally, an investor can sell at any time and receive the value of the shares.

Types of mutual funds include equity funds, index funds, and balance funds. Equity funds consist mainly of stocks. These stocks can come from small, medium, or large companies. Index funds include stocks that correspond to major stock indices, like the Standard & Poor's (S&P) 500, and balance funds include both stocks and bonds. Investors' decisions for funds are also based on investment strategies, including the following:

- **Aggressive growth** includes stocks with above-average growth.

- **Income oriented** includes investment tools, like bonds and dividend-paying stocks, that pay out steady returns on a regular basis.
- **Value investing** includes stocks that are selling for less than they should be and will most likely take a long time to rise.

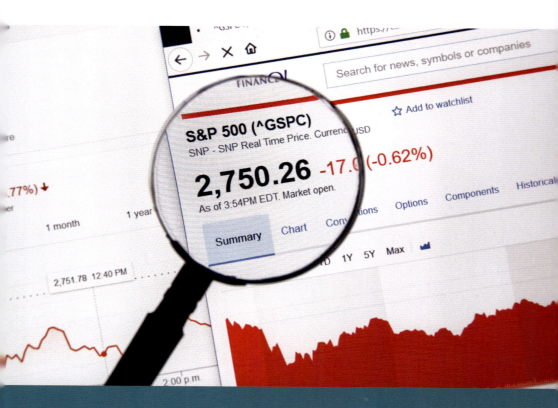

Index funds are safe investments made up of stocks that closely match a market index such as the Standard & Poor's 500, which tracks some of the largest US companies.

Leaders in the technology industry converge to discuss next-generation financial services at the 2019 Bridge Forum conference in San Francisco, California.

Investors with the best strategies for choosing mutual funds will likely be those who take into account their tolerance for risk and their longstanding investing goals.

SECTOR FUNDS

Investors may choose to concentrate their investments in a certain sector or industry, which is known as a sector fund. For example, natural resource funds focus primarily on oil and gas, while utility funds focus on gas and electricity. Real estate funds involve real estate, or property with land and buildings. Investors choosing financial funds have portfolios which consist of insurance, banking, and mortgage-related stocks. Health care funds incorporate businesses such as pharmaceutical companies. Investors can also put their money into technology funds, which include products and services relating to computers, software, and information technology. Precious metals funds invest in mining operations and other companies dealing in gold, silver, copper, and other metals. There are even sector funds that focus on consumer staples, like food and tobacco, and consumer cyclicals, such as cars and entertainment-related stocks.

If an investor predicts that a specific industry is going to experience an increase in its stock prices, he or she can buy a sector fund that has stocks from several companies in that industry. This action is a means of diversifying within a sector. Suppose an investor wants to buy stock in a technology company. The investor has options. Option A is having the investor buy stock from only one technology company. Option B is having the investor buy a sector fund, with stocks in several technology companies. If the company from Option A does not do well, then the investor can potentially lose some of the original investment money. But if he or she chose Option B, then some of this loss may be offset by increases in the stock prices of the other companies in the sector fund.

Choosing a sector fund can also depend on investment strategy. For example, technology funds are usually chosen by those who favor aggressive growth. Conversely, investors who believe that the economy is going to enter a recession or downturn may choose utility sector funds, which focus on goods and services that are essential. People will need to pay for utilities even when the economy is struggling.

5 PLAYING THE MARKET

You've probably heard business news reports discussing "markets" or "the market." Maybe the commentator mentions that "the market is down," or "markets have made up for losses earlier in the week." These markets refer to different stock markets, also known as stock exchanges, where stocks are traded.

When a company goes public, it chooses a market in which its stocks will be bought and sold. Every company has a unique ticker symbol—an abbreviation that identifies the stock on listings of current prices. Amazon is AMZN, for example, and Bank of America is BAC. Investors enter ticker symbols when making trades.

KNOW THE EXCHANGES

Stocks are bought and sold on many different markets across the world. Traditionally, the center of activity was the trading floor of a stock exchange building. Today, most trading is done electronically. In general, buying and selling on the stock market takes place between investors. You're not buying stock

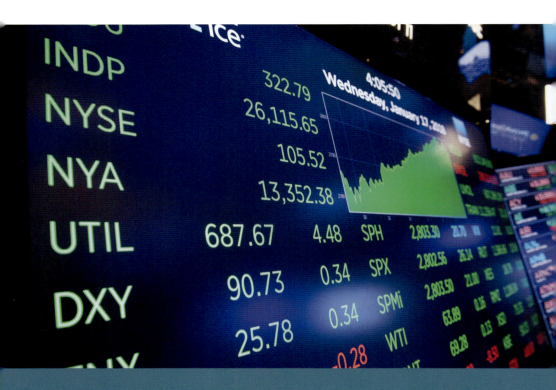

Stock market numbers are seen at the New York Stock Exchange on January 17, 2018, as stock market indices extended upward trends to close at record finishes.

from the company—you are buying it from a shareholder who is selling the stock. Companies don't regularly deal their own shares on the market.

In the United States, a general statement about performance of "the market" is probably referring to the New York Stock Exchange (NYSE). It is the oldest stock exchange in the United States and the largest in the world. Stock from more than 2,400 major companies is traded on the NYSE. To be listed, a company must have at least 1.1 million shares of outstanding stock and an income of over $10 million for the past three years according to *Investing 101*. Some of the major corporations that trade on the NYSE include ExxonMobil, General Electric, AT&T, and JPMorgan Chase.

The world's second largest stock exchange, with more than 3,000 listings, is the NASDAQ, also based in New York City. Many technology companies choose the NASDAQ when going public.

The Tokyo Stock Exchange in Tokyo, Japan, is the largest stock exchange in Asia and the fourth largest in the world, listing stocks such as Toyota and Mitsubishi.

Major companies on the NASDAQ include Apple, Google, and Facebook.

Investors may also look at opportunities on international markets. Financial centers abroad include London, Tokyo, Shanghai, Hong Kong, and cities in Europe that are part of the Euronext exchange.

Overall stock market performance can be gauged through values of stock market indices, which track a particular representative group of stocks to indicate overall trends. The best known stock market index is the Dow Jones Industrial Average (DJIA, or the Dow). The Dow follows thirty stocks of giant companies listed on the NYSE that are drawn from different sectors of the

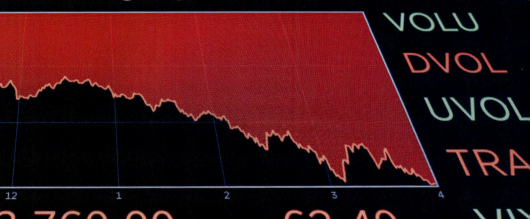

STOCK EXCHANGE

POST 6

4:06:36
February 2, 2018

NY

VOLU
DVOL
UVOL
TRA

12   1   2   3   4

2,760.00   -62.40   VI

2,762.13   -59.85   R

A display at the New York Stock Exchange shows the stock market numbers near the end of a trading day in which the Dow plunged more than 660 points.

economy. When a commentator states that the Dow rose by a certain number of points during a trading day, it means that overall, prices of the stocks listed in the index increased.

Another index is the NASDAQ Composite, which tracks all of the companies listed on the NASDAQ exchange. Because of the number of tech companies trading on NASDAQ, the NASDAQ Composite index provides a good indicator of performance in the tech sector. Investors also watch the Standard & Poor's 500 composite index, also known as the S&P 500. It follows a broad range of 500 stocks listed by large American companies in various sectors. It is considered a good indicator of performance of large-cap companies.

Stock market performance can be represented by stock market charts—graphs showing the rising and falling values of a particular index or of individual stocks. Investors can identify performance trends at a glance when evaluating a stock chart. Charts can be adjusted to show data over short-term or long-term periods. You could look at the ups and downs of a single day on the stock market or view the performance of a stock over the past decade.

INVESTING VERSUS SPECULATION

There's more than one strategy for making money on the stock market. Investors generally hold onto stocks for an extended period of time. They own them long enough to receive dividends or see the stock appreciate in value.

Stock traders approach the market with a different set of strategies and goals. Rather than seeking out stocks for their

BUBBLES AND BOOMS AND BUSTS

The stock market tends to move upward or downward in long-term periods that last for a year or more. Generally, the stock market suffers during a recession. Sometimes, stock market turmoil can be a factor in causing an economic downturn. A stock market bubble occurs when stock prices of a type of asset increase to levels much higher than the actual values. The stock market booms as investors race to invest in the asset, but eventually demand falters, prices plummet, and the

Unemployed men in Los Angeles, California, stand in line for soup and bread in 1930. Wages fell, unemployment rose, and homelessness increased during the Great Depression.

market crashes. The most notorious stock market crash began on October 24, 1929. Investors flocked to buy overpriced stocks during the "Roaring Twenties." After the market peaked, the public panicked and sold their shares, causing the market to plunge. The ensuing Great Depression lingered until 1939.

Stock market crashes are infrequent events. More often, the stock market experiences a correction. Prices decline, but not severely enough to qualify as a bear market. A correction may be followed by a rally—a sustained increase in stock prices.

value over the long term, traders focus on the price of a stock and the likelihood that it can yield a quick profit. They analyze different cycles of the market and predict which sectors are most likely to rise quickly. Traders may play the market with their own money through brokers, or they may work for a financial institution such as an investment bank.

Investors follow the quarterly earnings reports of their stocks and watch them grow over years. Traders hold onto their shares for days or perhaps months. Day traders buy and then sell stocks within hours or minutes during the period of a trading day. Trading is a relatively recent means of making money on the stock market, and it is made possible by technological developments. Today, traders can gather data about market trends instantaneously and react immediately by buying or selling.

A type of trading called high-frequency trading (HFT) utilizes electronic trading platforms to make a large number of fast trades. HFT requires powerful computers, fast connections, and algorithms that use mathematical models to analyze price changes and decide which stocks to buy or sell. A delay of just millionths of a second can make a difference in whether a trade is profitable or not. Most high-frequency trading is done by huge financial firms using supercomputers and top-secret algorithms.

The supercomputers that perform high frequency trading (HFT) process large numbers of transactions in fractions of a second, using complex algorithms to choose stocks to buy and sell.

Trading is more speculative than investing—traders may buy stocks that are considered high-risk on the expectation that their prices may rise and yield big short-term rewards. They try to anticipate the direction of price movements. Although speculating involves more risk than investing, it involves expertise and a set of strategies and tools used to determine when to buy and sell. Volatility makes investors nervous about the performance of their stocks. For traders, however, volatility can represent an opportunity to make a quick profit with a trade. If you're interested in trying out

DIAGNOSING THE ECONOMY

In addition to researching individual stocks and broader stock market trends, savvy investors should also pay attention to the overall health of the economy. Statistics called economic indicators measure economic activity and help predict the direction of the economy. The stock market itself is considered an economic indicator—it reflects the performance of big companies. Another key indicator, gross domestic product (GDP), measures how much a country's economy is growing. Statistics on job growth include data on the unemployment rate and earnings. Consumer price index (CPI) tracks changes in prices and indicates whether inflation is occurring. These economic indicators, among others, measure the strength of the economy and predict whether expansion or slowdown is likely to occur—data that could affect your stock portfolio decisions.

trading yourself, check out virtual trading tools that don't use real money.

TRICKS OF THE TRADE

Traders generally use different metrics for analyzing stocks than investors. Measurements that analyze a company's performance—such as P/E ratio and return on equity—are known as fundamental analysis. Traders tend to use another set of tools called technical analysis. Instead of focusing on value, technical analysis examines trends related to stock price and volume, which is the number of shares being traded during a certain time frame. A trader examines charts and graphs of a stock's price and uses indicators to predict the price movement based on past patterns. A moving average, for example, smoothes out fluctuations to provide a clear signal of a stock's direction. A couple more complex tools include the moving average convergence/divergence (MACD) and the stochastic oscillator. Technical analysis includes a wide range of tools that provide different insights into a stock's movement. It takes practice to pick which indicators to use, combine them, and interpret the results.

Traders also employ different tools and techniques for buying and selling. An investor chooses a stock, buys it, and holds it for a period of time. In a process called short selling, a seller can make money off of a stock without ever owning it. Traders attempt to short sell a stock when they believe that the price will fall. The trader borrows the stock from a broker and sells it. If the price drops, the trader buys it back at a lower price and returns it to the broker. Short selling is generally highly speculative and risky.

Trading can involve financial tools and products that are more complex than stocks or bonds being bought and sold outright. In trading financial instruments called derivatives, for example, the trader does not own the underlying asset, which can be stocks or other areas, such as commodities or currencies. A few common types of derivatives include swaps, stock options, and futures contracts.

Whether you make money on the market as an investor or trader, you are required to pay taxes on your earnings. Some investors and traders time their investments to

Traders are seen on the floor of the New York Stock Exchange on June 18, 2015, during the initial public offering (IPO) of the fitness technology company Fitbit.

minimize the taxes they must pay. In some cases, expenses related to investments may be tax deductible.

Anyone interested in stocks should set financial goals and research the best strategy for yielding a good return. You may discover that you're fascinated by putting together a great portfolio or that you're a natural at predicting stock price trends based on charts. Even if you're not interested in actively investing or trading, understanding stocks is a key aspect of financial literacy. This knowledge is essential for managing your money and keeping up with economic trends.

GLOSSARY

appreciate To increase in value or number over time.

asset Something possessing value that can be used to generate income.

bear market A downward trend in which stock prices overall drop by at least 20 percent for two months or more.

bond A type of fixed interest investment based on debt issued by governments or public companies.

brokerage A company that buys and sells stocks or other assets for an investor.

bull market An upward trend in which stock prices rise for a sustained period of time.

capital Financial resources that a company can use to generate growth in ways such as buying goods used to increase production.

commission An amount of money paid to an agent for conducting a transaction.

corporation A type of organization that can act as a legal entity separate from its owners.

debt Money owed to another.

diversify To invest in a broad range of types of assets.

dividend Money paid to shareholders out of company profits.

dividend yield A stock's yearly dividend payment expressed as a percentage of the stock's price.

equity For shareholders, equity is a company's total assets minus its total liabilities, or debt.

initial public offering (IPO) The first time the corporation issues stock.

interest The cost of borrowing money or return on an investment.

invest To put money into something to receive a financial return.

mutual fund A security that combines investors' money and then allocates it into different investments.

profit Money earned by a business after paying all costs of making and selling its products or services.

return Profit or loss on an investment.

revenue Money earned by a company.

risk The amount of uncertainty related to potential loss in making an investment decision.

sector A distinct area of the economy.

security A financial instrument such as a stock or bond that possesses value and can be traded.

shareholder An individual who owns stock in a company.

stock An investment that represents an ownership share in a corporation.

stock exchange A financial marketplace where securities such as stocks and bonds are bought and sold.

stock market index A measurement of the performance of a section of the stock market for a comparison of the returns on investments. Standard & Poor's 500 is an index of the 500 largest US publicly traded companies, for example.

Bank of Canada

234 Wellington Street

Ottawa, ON K1A 0G9

Canada

(800) 303-1282

Website: https://www.bankofcanada.ca

Twitter: @bankofcanada

The Bank of Canada is Canada's central bank, which is charged with maintaining stable financial markets among other duties.

Canadian Securities Administrators (CSA)

CSA Secretariat

Tour de la Bourse

800, Square Victoria, Suite 2510

Montreal, QC H4Z 1J2

Canada

(514) 864-9510

Website: https://www.securities-administrators.ca

Facebook: @CSA.ACVM

Twitter: @CSA_News

The CSA provides protection to Canadian investors and manages regulation of Canadian capital markets.

Federal Reserve System

20th Street and Constitution Avenue NW

Washington, DC 20551

(202) 452-3000

Website: https://www.federalreserve.gov; https://www.
stlouisfed.org/education/tools-for-enhancing-the-
stock-market-game-invest-it-forward/episode-1-
understanding-capital-markets

Facebook and Twitter: @federalreserve

The Federal Reserve is the central bank of the United States.
The St. Louis branch of the Federal Reserve provides an
overview of capital markets, along with educational tools.

Investor.gov

US Securities and Exchange Commission

Office of Investor Education and Advocacy

100 F Street NE

Washington, DC 20549

(800) 732-0330

Website: https://www.investor.gov

Facebook: @SECInvestorEducation

Twitter: @SEC_Investor_Ed

Investor.gov provides Americans with resources on making
good investment decisions and protecting themselves
from fraud.

MarketWatch

Dow Jones & Co.

1211 Avenue of the Americas

New York, NY 10036

(212) 597-5600
Website: https://www.marketwatch.com
Facebook, Twitter, and Instagram: @MarketWatch
Published by Dow Jones & Co., MarketWatch provides
    business, finance, and stock market news.

New York Stock Exchange (NYSE)
11 Wall Street
New York, NY 10005
(212) 656-3000
Website: https://www.nyse.com
Facebook, Twitter, and Instagram: @NYSE
The New York Stock Exchange, located on Wall Street in
    New York City, is the world's largest trading exchange
    based on dollar volume. It is also sometimes called the
    Big Board.

US Department of the Treasury
1500 Pennsylvania Avenue NW
Washington, DC 20220
(202) 622-2000
Website: https://home.treasury.gov
Twitter: @USTreasury
Instagram: @TreasuryDept
The US Department of the Treasury manages federal
    finances by collecting taxes, overseeing the public debt,
    paying bills, and issuing all US money.

US Securities and Exchange Commission (SEC)
SEC Headquarters
100 F Street NE
Washington, DC 20549
(800) 732-0330
Website: https://www.sec.gov
Facebook: @SECInvestorEducation
Twitter: @SEC_News
The SEC is the government agency that oversees
markets and protects investors' interests by enforcing
securities laws.

FOR FURTHER READING

Bianchi, David W. *Blue Chip Kids: What Every Child (and Parent) Should Know About Money, Investing, and the Stock Market*. Hoboken, NJ: Wiley, 2015.

Burkholder, Steve. *I Want More Pizza: Real World Money Skills for High School, College, and Beyond*. Encinitas, CA: Overcome Publishing, 2017.

Butler, Tamsen. *The Complete Guide to Personal Finance: For Teenagers and College Students*. Ocala, FL: Atlantic Publishing, 2019.

Currie, Stephen. *Teen Guide to Saving and Investing*. San Diego, CA: ReferencePoint Press, 2017.

Doyle, Nancy. *Manage Your Financial Life: Just Starting Out*. Glencoe, IL: The Doyle Group, 2018.

Hardyman, Robyn. *Understanding Stocks and Investing*. New York, NY: PowerKids Press, 2018.

Lowry, Erin. *Broke Millennial Takes On Investing: A Beginner's Guide to Leveling Up Your Money*. New York, NY: TarcherPerigee, 2019.

McGuire, Kara. *Making Money Work: The Teens' Guide to Saving, Investing, and Building Wealth*. North Mankato, MN: Compass Point Books, 2015.

Peterson, Judy Monroe. *Smart Strategies for Investing Wisely and Successfully*. New York, NY: Rosen Publishing, 2015.

Raskin, Ellen. *The Westing Game*. New York, NY: Puffin, 2018.

Tyson, Eric. *Personal Finance in Your 20s & 30s for Dummies*. Hoboken, NJ: John Wiley & Sons, 2018.

Uhl, Xina M., and Jeri Freedman. *Managing Bank Accounts and Investments*. New York, NY: Rosen Publishing, 2020.

Weeks, Marcus, and Derek Braddon. *Heads Up Money*. New York, NY: DK Publishing, 2017.

BIBLIOGRAPHY

Amadeo, Kimberly. "How the Stock Market Works." The Balance, March 13, 2019. https://www.thebalance .com/how-does-the-stock-market-work-3306244.

Backman, Maurie. "Stocks for Beginner Investors." The Motley Fool, April 27, 2018. https://www.fool.com/retirement /2018/04/27/stocks-for-beginner-investors.aspx.

Cagan, Michele. *Investing 101: From Stocks and Bonds to ETFs and IPOs, an Essential Primer on Building a Profitable Portfolio*. Avon, MA: Adams Media, 2016.

Cox, Jeff. "GE Shares Plunge 7% for Biggest Decline Since Housing Recession After Turnaround Plan Unveiled." CNBC, November 13, 2017. https://www.cnbc.com /2017/11/13/ge-announces-broad-restructuring-to -keep-health-care-aviation-and-energy-units.html.

Duggan, Wayne. "8 Stocks That American Teenagers Love." *U.S. News and World Report*, November 12, 2018. https:// money.usnews.com/investing/stock-market-news /slideshows/8-stocks-that-american-teenagers-love.

Epstein, Lita, and Grayson D. Roze. *Trading for Dummies*. 4th ed. Hoboken, NJ: Wiley, 2017.

Fiegerman, Seth. "5 Years After Rocky IPO, Facebook is Stronger than Ever." CNN, May 18, 2017. https:// money.cnn.com/2017/05/18/technology/facebook -ipo-anniversary/index.html.

Hayes, Adam. "Factors of Production." Investopedia. Retrieved April 23, 2019. https://www.investopedia .com/terms/f/factors-production.asp.

Hayes, Adam. "Price-to-Earnings Ratio (P/E Ratio) Definition." Investopedia. Retrieved April 20, 2019. https://www.investopedia.com/terms/p/price -earningsratio.asp.

Hayes, Adam. "Stock Basics Tutorial." Investopedia, May 25, 2017. https://www.investopedia.com/university/stocks.

Kelly, Jason. *The Neatest Little Guide to Stock Market Investing*. 5th ed. New York, NY: Plume, 2013.

Kemp, Michael. *Uncommon Sense: Investment Wisdom Since the Stock Market's Dawn*. Hoboken, NJ: Wiley, 2016.

Kennon, Joshua. "Investing for Beginners Basics: How to Calculate Stock Market Capitalization and Why It Is Important." The Balance, July 31, 2018. https://www .thebalance.com/stock-market-capitalization -101-357337.

Kennon, Joshua. "Using the Price-to-Earnings Ratio as a Quick Way to Value a Stock." The Balance, January 20, 2019. https://www.thebalance.com/using-price-to -earnings-356427.

Kline, Daniel B. "High Schools Fail at Teaching Personal Finance, Millennials Say." The Motley Fool, February 21, 2019. https://www.fool.com/investing/2019/02/21 /high-schools-fail-at-teaching-personal-finance -mil.aspx.

Korosec, Kirsten. "Spotify's First Day Trading Delivers $26.5 Billion Market Value." *Fortune*, April 3, 2018. http://fortune.com/2018/04/03/spotify-trading -market-cap.

Kutz, Steven. "This is the Most Innovative Financial Literacy Program in the US—It Gives Students Paychecks and Helps Them Open Bank Accounts." MarketWatch, May 9, 2019. https://www.marketwatch.com/story/how -one-high-school-is-teaching-hundreds-of-students-to -become-millionaires-2019-05-03.

Mladjenovic, Paul. *Stock Investing for Dummies*. 5th ed. Hoboken, NJ: Wiley, 2016.

Reuters. "Lyft Was Valued at $24.3 Billion in Its IPO, and Raised More than It Planned." VentureBeat, March 29, 2019. https://venturebeat.com/2019/03/29/lyft-was -valued-at-24-3-billion-in-its-ipo-and-raised-more -than-it-planned.

"What Is a Bear Market?" The Motley Fool. Retrieved May 5, 2019. https://www.fool.com/knowledge-center /bear-market.aspx.

White, John. *Investing in Stocks and Shares: A Step-By-Step Guide to Making Money on the Stock Market*. London, UK: Robinson, 2016.

INDEX

T

target share price, 16
technical analysis, 61
ticker symbols, 51
total return, 22
trade commission, 35
trends, as investment predictors, 24

U

Uber, 10
Uniform Gift to Minors Act /
    Uniform Transfer to Minors Act,
    36

V

value, variation in, 21
value investing, 47
value stocks, 30
VF Corporation, 24
Visa, 11
voting rights, for shareholders, 11

W

Walmart, 10
websites, purchasing stocks from,
    29

Y

yield, 18, 19, 20, 23, 27, 28, 46, 58,
    60

ABOUT THE AUTHORS

Corona Brezina is an author who has written more than a dozen books for young adults. Several of her previous books have also focused on government, social, and economic topics, including *Understanding Equal Rights; How Imports and Exports Work;* and *Understanding the Federal Reserve and Monetary Policy*. She lives in Chicago, Illinois.

Barbara Gottfried is an economics and personal finance content developer. She has written several books for young adults on finance-related topics, including *Top 10 Secrets for Investing Successfully; Top 10 Secrets for Spending Your Money Wisely;* and *Paying for College: Practical, Creative Strategies*. She lives in Brookline, Massachusetts.

PHOTO CREDITS